Flicker

What the wind left behind...

Jyotsna D

BookLeaf Publishing

India | USA | UK

Copyright © Jyotsna D
All Rights Reserved.

This book has been self-published with all reasonable efforts taken to make the material error-free by the author. No part of this book shall be used, reproduced in any manner whatsoever without written permission from the author, except in the case of brief quotations embodied in critical articles and reviews.

The Author of this book is solely responsible and liable for its content including but not limited to the views, representations, descriptions, statements, information, opinions, and references ["Content"]. The Content of this book shall not constitute or be construed or deemed to reflect the opinion or expression of the Publisher or Editor. Neither the Publisher nor Editor endorse or approve the Content of this book or guarantee the reliability, accuracy, or completeness of the Content published herein and do not make any representations or warranties of any kind, express or implied, including but not limited to the implied warranties of merchantability, fitness for a particular purpose.

The Publisher and Editor shall not be liable whatsoever...

Made with ❤ on the BookLeaf Publishing Platform
www.bookleafpub.in
www.bookleafpub.com

Dedication

For those who love deeply, break quietly and rise again... in verses only they understand...

Preface

Flicker - "between certainty and doubt, joy and sorrow, holding on and letting go. Between light and shadow - the quiet hesitations and the lingering echoes."

These 'moments in words' freeze the fleeting ruminations, scream the whispers lost to time, and sear the burning ache of straggling thought!

In the ephemeral glow of love, loss and longing, ***"Flicker" is both spark... and silence!*** - an aide-memoire that even evanescent light can leave a sempiternal imprint.

Acknowledgements

*To the silence that held my words before
they were spoken.
To the shadows that shaped my thoughts in
the quiet corners of time.
To the fugacious moments that arrived
unannounced, left their echoes, and never
returned.
To the unseen hands that guided me,
whether through absence or presence.*

This book is a collection of everything that
has lingered—whispers, wounds, wonders...

**If these words find a home in another heart,
then they have done what they were meant
to do...**

Melodies of Silence

The lyrics, they are written,
The music is composed,
In harmony, they are smitten,
Each note disclosed.

So vivid, every verse,
With rhythm, rhyme, and flow,
Each sound so diverse,
Engulfing emotions, oh so slow.

I stand for a rendition,
Of a beautiful tale of love,
There's just silence, no emotion,
That speaks volumes, somehow.

I try to fathom the truth,
And I can't pretend not to know,
That there's no story that can be told,
'Cause my voice goes where you go!

Heartstrings

In the quiet of the morning light,
When dawn's first colors softly bite,
My thoughts, they only drift to you,
A silent whisper in a sky so blue.

Each day, it seems a little longer,
My heart grows fonder, feelings stronger,
The empty spaces by my side,
Are filled with images of your smile.

The laughter shared, the stories told,
The gentle warmth, need your hand to hold,
I miss the way you light my days,
In countless, sweet and tender ways.

The world moves on, but I'm still here,
Held captive by your memories dear,
A silent wish with every star,
To bridge the gap, no matter how far.

Until the day we're together again,
Know that I'll never be sane,
My heart is only tied to you,
I miss you deeply, through and through.

Strength in the Storm

Oh, my dear, I see your pain,
Your heart weighs heavy in the rain.
But know that clouds won't last for long,
You're made of courage, bold and strong.

The world feels harsh, the days unfair,
But love surrounds you everywhere.
In every tear, I see your fight,
And I know you'll rise, reclaim your light.

It's okay to feel, to bend, to cry,
Emotions pass like birds that fly.
But here I am, right by your side,
In me, you've always got a guide.

So rest, my love, and take your time,
Your strength will grow, your stars will shine.
Though now it's hard, this too will end,
And brighter days will start again.

Caged Heart

I've been lied to, broken, left to bleed,
Trust is a luxury I no longer need.
The words I hear, I weigh with doubt,
Too many times, they've turned inside out.

This is who I am, guarded and wary,
The past I hold is heavy to carry.
You can try to stay, or walk away,
But I'll not beg, either way.

If you choose me, know what's true,
I'll fight the world to death, for you.
Yet this heart is mine to shield, defend,
And you can leave --- if this is the end.

Whispers from Above

From beyond where stars reside,
I watch you, son, with boundless pride.
Each step you take, each choice you make,
I'm guiding you for love's own sake.

May courage fill your waking days,
May kindness light your chosen ways.
I send you strength when trials arise,
And wisdom, clear as morning skies.

Go forth, my child, with heart so true,
For all I was, now lives in you.
With every dawn, may joy impart,
The gift of peace, a steady start.

Fear of Falling

I'm scared of getting close,
As my heart definitely knows.
The searing pain when we are away,
How do I explain, what can I say?

I try so hard to keep my peace,
But pain like this will never cease.
A silent storm I hide inside,
In shadows where my feelings bide.

I want to hold you, pull you near,
But all I taste is empty fear.
So I stay distant, out of sight,
To keep my heart from aching tonight.

Yet every beat still calls your name,
A gentle spark that fuels the flame.
I love you more than words can say,
But loving means, I'll stay away.

Unwoven Ties

In the quiet of this aching night,
I release your hand, let go the fight.
For in the end, love's gentle art,
Is learning when to mend a heart.

Tears fall like rain on a barren field,
A heart once open, now must shield.
Memories linger, like shadows they stay,
Haunting the nights, tainting the day.

Cherish the lessons, release the pain,
Embrace the sunshine, dance in the rain.
For though our paths have come undone,
I know your journey has just begun.

Infinite Love

I love you like the stars love the night,
Shining brightly, casting a guiding light.
I love you like the ocean loves the shore,
Endlessly reaching, always wanting more.

I love you like the sun loves the day,
Warming the world in its gentle way.
I love you like the flowers love the rain,
Thriving and blooming, easing the pain.

With every beat of my heart,
This love will be true,
Forever and always,
I'll cherish you.

Unpolished

I trace the edges of my flaws,
Sharp, stubborn, unmoved by time,
You ask me to shift, to loosen, to laugh,
But this is the only shape that's mine.

I have tried to sand my rough edges,
Whispered promises into the wind,
But the storm inside me rages on,
Pulling me back to who I have always been.

It's not defiance, not indifference,
Just the weight of being me,
A puzzle piece that won't quite fit,
No matter how hard I try.

Still, my heart is yours, unchanged and whole,
To give you a different version of me, it's tough.
All I can give you is love so fierce and yes, my soul,
If only that were enough.

Goodbye, Gently

I shed a tear for us,
For there's not going to be one.
This relationship that was built of trust,
Built only to be torn.

The laughter we shared now echoes away,
Lost in the silence of words left unspoken.
Our promises, once bright as the day,
Lie shattered like glass, forever broken.

The warmth of your touch, a fading memory,
A ghost of the love that we used to know.
Now I walk alone through this cruel reverie,
Trying to let go, but struggling so.

I shed a tear for the future we'd planned,
For the dreams that will never take flight.
Our story is ending, the ink leaves my hand,
And fades into the stillness of night.

Yet deep in my heart, you'll always remain,
A part of the person I've grown to be.
Though our chapter ends, the lessons remain,
And I'll cherish the good, though you're not with me.

More Than Words

In the quiet moments of the day,
When the world feels far away,
I think of you and all you do,
And my heart is filled with gratitude.

Your kindness shines in every deed,
Your love is all I will ever need,
Through highs and lows, you are always there,
With gentle words and tender care.

You are my rock, my guiding light,
In your arms, the world feels right,
Thank you for the love you show,
My blessing you are, more than you know.

Each day with you is a precious gift,
Even though to receive, I am unfit,
For all the joy and all the laughter,
Thank you now and ever after.

Fading Valentine

The roses wilt before they bloom,
Candles flicker, dim with gloom.
Valentine's wrapped in quiet goodbyes,
Love dissolves in tired sighs.

No roses sweet can change the taste,
Of all we lost, of love misplaced.
No whispered words, no last embrace,
Can turn this hurt to something safe.

So let the hearts and ribbons fall,
Let silence answer every call.
Not all love stories end with light,
Some fade away on Valentine's night.

To Many More

A year has passed, where has time flown,
From seeds of love, how we've both grown.
Through highs and lows, magic we did find,
We built a bond, heart, soul, and mind.

The days we've shared, with words unsaid,
Woven with joy, with love that led.
In silent glances, or laughter's gleam,
We chase our hopes, fulfil our dream.

The first of many, this year we claim,
To eternity, a steady flame.
Here's to the future, the days ahead,
As in the path of love, we gently tread.

To us again, one year complete,
With every heartbeat, happiness we greet.
Through time, together, we'll continue to stand,
Side by side, hand in hand.

Echoes of Regret

I'm sorry that I hurt you,
That's not what I meant to do.
I feel like I don't deserve the love
That you show me, so true.

I'm sorry for what I'm putting you through,
The pain and tears, I deeply rue.
I'll strive to make amends, too,
Hoping to strengthen the trust between us two.

I wish I could turn back time,
To undo and erase the pain.
Your forgiveness I truly seek,
I'm hoping we can start anew again.

But do know that I love you,
And no matter what I do,
My heart remains steadfast and true,
Forever cherishing the moments with you.

Dawn of Hope

There's a blanket over me,
A heavy dark one at that.
Through it, nothing I can see,
Can't think of who I can be.

It's as heavy as my heart,
That's being shredded apart.
I can't find the reason why,
Doesn't make sense, I, Me, My?

What am I holding on to?
There's no hope left.
Holding tight to shadows cast,
Lost in questions from the past.

I search for a guiding light,
To break through this endless night,
And in this, the darkest hour,
Does hope have any power?

It's now buried deep and low,
Will it rise to brightly glow?
With each dawn, a chance to find,
Strength anew, a clearer mind.

Though the blanket weighs me down,
I hope it will lift me off the ground.

Eternal Embrace

I love you so much,
I can't explain enough.
Every smile, every touch,
Without you, it's so tough.

I want to feel the warmth you bring,
Like the first days of spring.
In your arms, I'm at ease,
A gentle whisper in the breeze.

You're the light in my dark,
In my soul, a permanent mark.
With you, life's a gorgeous dance,
Every moment, a new chance.

To laugh, to love, to grow,
Together, perfect, is all I want.
And whatever happens, I need you to know,
Without you, live, I can't!

Farewell, My Love

Our paths crossed and intertwined,
Through moments cherished and times shined.
But now the time has come to part,
To let go and protect your heart.

We've laughed, cried, grown so much,
I'll miss your smile, I'll miss your touch.
The love we shared, a treasured phase,
Now fades into these wistful days.

The future calls with voices clear,
It's time to face what we both fear.
No hurt, no anger, no feelings at all,
Our love is real, but not fate's call.

May you find joy in what's ahead,
And think of us with love unsaid.
Goodbye, my love, our journey ends,
I don't think we will survive as friends.

Hate, Love and Everything In Between

I hate you like the sun hates the night,
A strong feud, never ending, never right.
I hate you like the storm hates the calm,
A clash of forces, causing endless harm.

I hate you like the desert hates the rain,
Yearning for relief, yet feeling only pain.
I hate you like the fire hates the cold,
A burning intensity that never grows old.

But deep down inside, it's clear to see,
Beneath all the hate, there's a part of me,
That longs for your touch, the warmth of your love,
I wish you were with me here and now.

Moments in Time

Many loving months have passed,
Moments woven, memories amassed.
From the first hello to this day,
We've found love in every way.

Through the storms and the sunshine bright,
You've been my peace, my guiding light.
Every smile, every tear we've shared,
Shows how deeply we've both cared.

With each heartbeat, I've grown to see,
The beauty of us, endlessly.
Here's to many more months to come,
Our love a journey, just begun.

Happy anniversary, my love so true,
Here's to forever --- me and you.

Through Every Storm

I don't envy you, with work so steep,
Mountains of tasks, I wish you peaceful sleep.
But know you're doing something right,
You rise, you push, you stay in fight.

The weight you bear, I see it clear,
But I am here, I love you dear.
Your strength, your stride—they're shining through,
And when you're tired, I'm here for you.

So take a breath, let worries fade,
Lean on me—I'll help, I'm made,
To help lighten your load, to ease the strain,
Together we will kill this pain.

Crossroads of Pain

I shed today a silent tear,
Masked in it anxiety and fear.
The pain pushing from deep within,
I feel like I am committing a sin.

To one I give the hope of life,
To the other I have to take the knife.
And stuck in between is a pure soul,
The one that makes me feel so whole.

How do I sort this mess out?
How do I erase this self-doubt?
How do I get away from the pain?
Do I take my life? I cry in vain.

Oh, how do I grow strong in this?
I want to just embrace death's kiss.
I just need something to hold on to,
Faith, love to pull me through.

Just You, Just Me

I can't help but smile,
At the little things you do,
The way you hum a tune so soft,
As your laughter echoes too.

The way your fragrance fills the air,
Like sunshine breaking through the rain,
A fleeting glance, a gentle touch,
That soothes away the deepest pain.

I can't help but smile,
When you call my name just right,
In your presence, time slows down,
And everything else feels so light.

I can't help but smile,
When we hold hands and just be,
No need for words, no rush of time,
Just you, just me, just free.

Incomplete

I miss you like the desert misses the rain,
Like faded memory calling in vain.
I miss you like the stars miss the night,
Like the darkness misses the morning light.

I miss you like the ocean misses the shore,
Like a heart that longs for more.
I miss you like a book misses its words,
Like the sky misses the birds.

I miss you like a mother misses her child,
Like flowers that miss the wild.
I miss you like my heart would miss a beat,
Like a story, untold, incomplete.

Regret

If I had known this would be the last,
I would have held your hand a little longer,
Spoken the words unspoken,
Mended gaps, made the bond stronger.

I would have traced your footsteps, fearing you would
go,
Let my eyes linger on your smile,
Savoured laughter, embraced pain, so you know,
If I had known, if have stayed a while.

If only I had known, I would have slowed time,
Etching in my heart, that you will always be mine,
For now all I have, is just echoes of memories,
And the longing to relive them once again.

More than Existence

To be held, is it too much to ask,
To love, is it too much of a task?
To listen, time is all we need,
To feel, the hearts silent creed.

To care, a soul don't you have?
To trust, a bond I might suggest,
To dream, of a future untold,
To hope, for stories to unfold.

To mend, all that's broken,
To believe, all that's unspoken,
To weave, a path of memories,
To leave, enviable histories.

To live, not merely exist,
To save, only all the moments missed,
To give, so our souls connect,
To cherish, every moment, Oh so Perfect!

www.ingramcontent.com/pod-product-compliance
Lightning Source LLC
Chambersburg PA
CBHW061321140726
47998CB00006B/2495